Speak Up!

Kelly Doudna

Consulting Editor, Diane Craig, M.A./Reading Specialist

Published by ABDO Publishing Company, 4940 Viking Drive, Edina, Minnesota 55435.

Printed in the United States.

Credits
Edited by: Pam Price
Curriculum Coordinator: Nancy Tuminelly
Cover and Interior Design and Production: Mighty Media
Photo Credits: AbleStock, BananaStock Ltd., Hemera, Rubberball Productions, ShutterStock

Library of Congress Cataloging-in-Publication Data

Doudna, Kelly, 1963-
    Speak up! / Kelly Doudna.
      p. cm. -- (Character concepts)
    ISBN-13: 978-1-59928-741-6
    ISBN-10: 1-59928-741-2
    1. Oral communication--Juvenile literature. I. Title.

P95.D687 2007
302.2'2242--dc22
                                                                    2006032295

SandCastle™ books are created by a professional team of educators, reading specialists, and content developers around five essential components—phonemic awareness, phonics, vocabulary, text comprehension, and fluency—to assist young readers as they develop reading skills and strategies and increase their general knowledge. All books are written, reviewed, and leveled for guided reading, early reading intervention, and Accelerated Reader® programs for use in shared, guided, and independent reading and writing activities to support a balanced approach to literacy instruction.

Let Us Know

SandCastle would like to hear your stories about reading this book. What is your favorite page? Was there something hard that you needed help with? Share the ups and downs of learning to read. We want to hear from you! To get posted on the ABDO Publishing Company Web site, send us e-mail at:

sandcastle@abdopublishing.com

SandCastle Level: Transitional

Speak Up!*

Your character is a part of who you are. It is how you act when you go somewhere. It is how you get along with other people. It is even what you do when no one is looking!

You show character when you speak up. You talk clearly so that others understand you. You listen when other people have something to say. You don't mumble when you tell your dad about school!

Emma is learning how to make pancakes. She doesn't interrupt her dad. Emma listens to what he has to say.

Kim faces her grandma while they talk. Kim tells her about her summer. Kim speaks up.

Kelly's mom is on a business trip. She calls Kelly on the phone. Kelly speaks clearly. She uses proper language.

Ethan talks to his grandpa about baseball. He speaks in a clear voice. He talks slowly. Ethan speaks up.

Jack tells his sisters
about his day at school.
Jack doesn't use bad
words. Jack uses proper
language.

Speak Up!

Olivia's whole family
is together for dinner.
Olivia speaks up and
sounds like a winner.

16

Aunt Carmen asks
about soccer,
Olivia's favorite sport.
Olivia looks right
at her and gives
the full report.

Olivia chats with
her cousin Juan,
whom she hasn't
seen since July.
She doesn't interrupt
his story while
she waits to reply.

Olivia talks to
her grandfather
and remembers
to speak clearly.
Grandpa's hard
of hearing,
and Olivia loves
him dearly!

Did You Know?

President Calvin Coolidge had the first official presidential speechwriter. That was the beginning of the Office of Speechwriting.

The talking stick has its origin in Native American culture. In a group of people, whoever holds the talking stick is allowed to speak uninterrupted.

Speaking in public is the number one fear reported by people in the United States.

Glossary

business – work done to earn a living.

clearly – in a way that is easily heard, seen, or understood.

interrupt – to break in while someone else is speaking.

language – the words people use to communicate.

mumble – to speak in a way that is hard to understand.

proper – correct and suitable.

report – a spoken or written story telling the details about something.

About SandCastle™

A professional team of educators, reading specialists, and content developers created the SandCastle™ series to support young readers as they develop reading skills and strategies and increase their general knowledge. The SandCastle™ series has four levels that correspond to early literacy development in young children. The levels are provided to help teachers and parents select appropriate books for young readers.

Emerging Readers
(no flags)

Beginning Readers
(1 flag)

Transitional Readers
(2 flags)

Fluent Readers
(3 flags)

These levels are meant only as a guide. All levels are subject to change.

To see a complete list of SandCastle™ books and other nonfiction titles from ABDO Publishing Company, visit **www.abdopublishing.com** or contact us at: 4940 Viking Drive, Edina, Minnesota 55435 • 1-800-800-1312 • fax: 1-952-831-1632